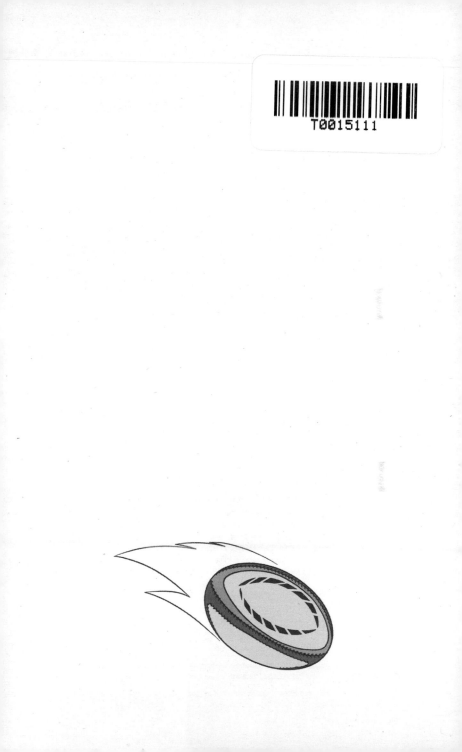

To Ian, Ben and Tom and their deep love of rugby.
C.G.

For all the kids in the world, this is just
a peek at the amazing things you can do.
L.A.

First published in Great Britain 2023 by Red Shed, part of Farshore

An imprint of HarperCollins*Publishers*
1 London Bridge Street, London SE1 9GF
www.farshore.co.uk

HarperCollins*Publishers*
Macken House, 39/40 Mayor Street Upper,
Dublin 1, D01 C9W8

ISBN 978 0 00 860612 1
Printed and bound in the UK using 100% Renewable Electricity at CPI Group (UK) Ltd.
001

A CIP catalogue record for this title is available from the British Library.

Stay safe online. Any website addresses listed in this book are correct at the time of going to print.
However, Farshore is not responsible for content hosted by third parties. Please be aware that online
content can be subject to change and websites can contain content that is unsuitable for children.
We advise that all children are supervised when using the internet.

MIX
Paper | Supporting
responsible forestry
FSC™ C007454

This book is produced from independently certified FSC™ paper
to ensure responsible forest management.

For more information visit: www.harpercollins.co.uk/green

INCREDIBLE
RUGBY

Written by Clive Gifford
Illustrations by Lu Andrade

RED■
SHED

"The whole point of rugby
is that it is, first and foremost,
a state of mind, a spirit."

– Jean-Pierre Rives,
34-times captain of the
French rugby union national team

Contents

Introduction

According to legend, rugby began when a schoolboy cheated at a game of football. It was 1823 and the boy was called William Webb-Ellis. He cheated by picking up the ball and running away with it! No one's certain if the story is true but William's school – Rugby School in Warwickshire – gave its name to an exciting new sport.

Rugby is now three sports – rugby union, rugby league and rugby sevens – and it's enjoyed not just in Britain but around the world. Rugby is played in more than 120 countries, from Argentina to Zimbabwe. More than 60 nations tried to qualify for the 2023 Rugby World Cup, a rugby union competition, held in France. This book is packed with tales of amazing achievements, inspirational players and extraordinary matches – as well as plenty of the sport's silliest moments!

Find out who scored a mind-blowing 152 points in a single match. Discover the pitch that has a tree growing out of the halfway line, the match that was interrupted by a kangaroo and the official who almost scored a try! From games played in Space and at the North Pole, to rotten refs and misbehaving mascots – we have it all!

You'll also find a glossary of key rugby terms, a simple guide to the rules of the game, plus player profiles and a quiz to test your knowledge.

So, wherever you are on your rugby journey, we hope you have fun!

PLAY!

"Rugby is a great game built on the foundation of respect and humility. It's about respecting one another."

– Maro Itoje

The First International

Did you know that rugby staged its first international match a year before football did?

In 1871, a crowd of more than 4,000 spectators in Edinburgh each paid 5p (worth just under £5 in today's money) to watch the first rugby match between countries – Scotland and England.

The rules were quite different to those of rugby union today. For starters, there were 20 players a side and the game lasted 100 not 80 minutes. There were no referees in charge of the game either. The players got on with it and if there was a dispute, they would go over to an umpire and argue! You didn't even get points for a try – you were simply awarded a 'try' at kicking a goal, which was worth a measly one point.

During the second half, Scotland's Angus Buchanan became the first try scorer in international rugby. William Cross kicked the goal after Angus's try to give Scotland a 1–0 win. The ball was tied up with ribbons and displayed proudly in a local shop for weeks afterwards! This game marked the start of a fierce rivalry that still runs today as the sides now compete for the Calcutta Cup trophy in the Six Nations Championship.

DID YOU KNOW?

Rugby league and rugby union have different rules, including the number of players in a team (15 in rugby union, 13 in rugby league) and the number of points scored for a try, drop kick or penalty. See page 165 for more infomation!

World Cup Whoops!

Even the greatest players make mistakes . . .

Sonny Bill Williams has won both Rugby Union and Rugby League World Cups with New Zealand. During the 2013 Rugby League World Cup game against Samoa, Sonny Bill broke through the Samoan defence and raced over the try line. But he didn't touch the ball down straight away – instead he slipped and his feet left the pitch, meaning that when he touched the ball down, no try was awarded. Huge embarrassment for the rugby legend but laughs for everyone else!

That's Snow Joke

Fun games of rugby have long been enjoyed in deep snow – diving for the try line is nice and soft. But in fact, snow rugby is a sport in its own right, with championships and rules that are different from the regular game.

The snowy pitch is 31m long and 25m wide, teams contain five players a side and matches are just ten minutes long. There are no line-outs or scrums and no kicking is allowed on the pitch. The aim, instead, is to pass and run to score a try, which is worth one point.

The sport is growing in popularity in Argentina, Russia and many countries in northern Europe. No snowballing your opponents allowed!

Prop With the Drop

In a wildly entertaining match between the Harlequins and Barbarians in 2022, Harlequins prop forward Joe Marler scored a try. Not content with throwing the ball to the regular goal kicker, the bulky prop added the conversion with a dainty drop kick that saw the ball sail between the posts. Harlequins ran out 73–28 winners.

DID YOU KNOW?

A 'Garryowen' is a high up-and-under kick made to give your team's chasers time to compete for the ball. It was named after an Irish rugby club, Garryowen FC, which used the tactic on their way to winning the Munster Senior Cup three years in a row, from 1924 to 1926.

Ledesma Lie-down

Mario Ledesma was a formidable front row forward from Argentina, who played 84 times for his country and then coached the national side between 2020 and 2022.

When coaching, Mario would sometimes like to view scrum practice from an unusual angle. He'd lie down on the grass in the tunnel formed by the two packs of forwards and gaze upwards at the players. Helpful? We have no idea!

You're Off!

No rugby player, league or union, wants the ref to show them a red card. Apart from their own match being over, it means they will leave their team one player short. Argentinean forward Tomás Lavanini is the only player in world rugby to have been shown the red card three times in international matches. He was first sent off in South Africa in 2017, then against England at the 2019 Rugby World Cup, and finally when playing Ireland in 2021. Naughty!

Try and Try Again

During a 1930 Wales versus Ireland game, two Welsh players, winger Howie Jones and forward Harry Peacock, both dived on the ball at the same time to score a try. The referee couldn't figure out who touched it down first so awarded it to both of them. Howie and Harry became the only joint try scorers in international rugby history!

DID YOU KNOW?

Respect for the referee at all times is something all codes of rugby are very proud of. When 18-year-old Australian Mark Meafua lost his temper and struck the referee, he was banned for ten years!

Coach Craig

Like many professional sports, rugby clubs hire and fire coaches regularly. Most current coaches in Australia's National Rugby League, for example, have been in charge of their side for only a season or two. This makes Craig Bellamy, head coach of the Melbourne Storm, quite an exception. He's been in charge of the club since 2003!

With 19 seasons under his belt, Craig has coached his team to more wins than defeats. As of the start of 2023, he's been in charge for 525 NRL games, winning 365 of them and drawing two. The Storm have won three Premierships and finished runners-up four times under his command.

The Game That Shook the World

The 2015 Rugby World Cup pitted Japan against the two-time world champions South Africa, aka the Springboks. Japan held an unwanted record – the most points conceded in a World Cup game: 145 (versus New Zealand in 1995). To make matters worse, they hadn't won a World Cup game for 24 years. Most pundits predicted a comfortable win for the Springboks and possibly a record thrashing for Japan.

They were oh-so wrong!

Japan, known as the Brave Blossoms, had a new-look team, coached by Eddie Jones, which was packed with flair and skill. According to Jones: "Japan can only play one way, we've got a little team, so we have to move the ball around and cause problems."

Everyone expected Japan to lose heavily at set pieces like the line-out and scrum. But the Brave Blossoms won all their own line-outs and sometimes challenged South Africa's. Across the pitch, they were sharp and made delicious passes and breaks, often started by their electric scrum half, Fumiaki Tanaka.

"The Japanese edge towards the posts . . . can they do it? They are close . . . oh YES! It looks like the skipper, Michael Leitch. What a hero as Japan hits the lead!"

– commentator

Full-back Ayumu Goromaru scored 24 points, but Japan had heroes all over the pitch. Captain Michael Leitch made a lung-busting 17 tackles and scored

Japan's first try. Kōsei Ono and Shota Horie charged around like tornadoes, while Amanaki Mafi used his strength to hold off the South African defenders.

But Japan did not have it all their own way. South Africa used their size and power to score four tries and, with ten minutes to go, the game was locked at a nail-biting 29–29. Handré Pollard then put the Springboks three points ahead with a penalty and many thought Japan's luck would end right there.

But the Brave Blossoms were having none of it. They pummelled the South African line and, as the game passed 80 minutes, the referee awarded Japan a penalty close to goal. If they kicked it, they would draw the match.

Now, though, Japan wanted more. They chose to

attack to score a winning try. A second penalty was awarded and, again, they chose to go for the win. With 84 minutes on the clock, Japan attacked again, spinning the ball across the pitch from right to left. Amanaki Mafi passed to Karne Hesketh, who dived over in the corner for the winning try. The crowd at Brighton's Amex Stadium erupted. Japan had triumphed 34–32!

> **"It was David versus Goliath but we have been training for this day for the last four years."**
> – Michael Leitch, captain

Japan would go on to win two more games at the 2015 tournament (against Samoa and USA). Then at the 2019 tournament, they defeated Ireland, Scotland, Samoa and Russia. The Brave Blossoms had arrived!

"This is the biggest upset in the World Cup, in any sport, EVER."
– Chris Rattue, *New Zealand Herald*

Double Dutch

The Netherlands women's rugby team was formed in 1982. That same year, they played the first ever official women's international versus France, losing 4–0 (at the time, you got four points, not five, for a try).

They certainly reversed that scoreline in their 2001 match against Belgium. The Dutch ran out 105–0 winners. Eleven years later, in 2012, the team were at it again, beating Finland by the exact same score. Double Dutch!

105–0 isn't even the Dutch women's team's highest ever score. That came in 2004 when they thrashed Denmark 141–3. Ouch!

Brilliant Bevan

Wigan and Hull FC were locked 0–0 after 13 minutes of their 2022 Super League game before Wigan winger Bevan French went berserk! He scored seven tries – in the 14th, 20th, 33rd, 38th, 43rd, 53rd and 55th minute – a Super League record. Wigan ran out easy winners, 60–0. Amazing!

DID YOU KNOW?

Only two countries have won the men's Rugby World Cup three times: New Zealand and South Africa, the defending champions before the 2023 tournament. And only two teams have reached the final and lost three times: England and France. Oops!

Red Roses Versus Black Ferns

In July 2019, in California, New Zealand's women's team (known as the Black Ferns) beat the England women's rugby union team, the Red Roses, 28–13. It turned out to be a turning point. Following this defeat, the Red Roses didn't lose another match in over three years.

Featuring the goal-kicking and line-breaking prowess of Emily Scarratt, the explosive power of Marlie Packer, and led by the inspirational back rower Sarah Hunter, the Red Roses were about to go on the rampage.

They thrashed the US team 89–0, Wales 73–7 and South Africa 75–0. Then in 2021, they got the chance for revenge against New Zealand, securing two outstanding victories.

But New Zealand would get the last laugh, defeating England 34–31 in the final of the 2022 Women's World Cup.

The Red Roses were devastated – but their record was one to be extremely proud of. Their 30-match winning streak is the longest ever in international rugby, for a men's or women's team (the men's rugby record is 24 matches, held by Cyprus). Impressive!

DID YOU KNOW?

In July 2022, the Fijiana – the Fijian women's rugby union team – handed out a thrashing to Papua New Guinea in the Oceania Championship. Fiji scored 24 tries to win 152–0 – the biggest international win ever recorded. A record-breaking 17 different players scored tries. Amazing!

Rugby Rituals

Many rugby players have routines or superstitions they like to stick to before a big game. Some happen when they enter the pitch – Jason Robinson used to like to run onto the pitch first whilst Australian legend David Campese insisted on going on last.

Joe Cokanasiga makes sure he touches all four corner flags of the pitch before the game kicks off whilst Ellis Genge always has a bath before an away game but not a home match!

Sydney Rabbitohs star Jai Arrow always starts to get ready precisely 37 minutes before his team begins their warm-up.

Rituals and superstitions often relate to a player's match-day kit. Irish fly half Jonny Sexton gets his kit prepared early, on a Thursday for a Saturday game. If she has had a good game previously, English back and goal-kicking legend Emily Scarratt will wear the same sports bra for the next game. And Emily has had a lot of good games as she's scored 640 points for England – a record.

John Smit played 111 Tests for South Africa, 82 of those as captain, leading his side to 2007 Rugby World Cup glory. On the day of the final and all his other games for South Africa, he would only wear black underpants under his shorts!

Breaking Down Barriers

Name: Hollie Davidson

Born: Aboyne, Scotland, 1992

Country: Scotland

Clubs: Murrayfield Wanderers

Position: Referee (formerly a scrum-half)

Famous for: World-class female referee officiating at women's and men's games

Hollie Davidson first got into rugby when she went with her class on school trips from their home town of Aboyne, near Aberdeen, to watch Scotland play in Edinburgh. "It was four hours each way," she recalled, "but the bus journeys were as fun as the game itself! We decided to put together a girls' team and that's where my passion for the game grew."

Along with her passion, Hollie's skill grew quickly too. Playing rugby union with Murrayfield Wanderers and the Scotland Under-20s team, she was a scrum-half and tenacious tackler. By 2012, aged 19, she was just five days away from her full Scotland debut.

But disaster struck when Hollie dislocated her shoulder. She was gutted – she couldn't make her Scottish debut. Worse still, doctors told her that the injury to her shoulder had caused permanent damage. Her dreams of rugby glory as a player had to be shelved.

But this setback was far from the end of Hollie's rugby career. She took up refereeing in 2015 and within months, it was clear that she would go far. Hollie was a natural. She became Scotland's first full-time female referee less than two years later.

It's been a whirlwind ride for Hollie ever since. In 2018, she refereed at the Commonwealth Games and the Rugby Europe International Championship. In 2019, she became the first woman to referee men's matches at the Melrose Sevens (see p104). Then, in 2021, she found herself in Tokyo, refereeing matches at the Olympics, as well as being in charge of men's matches in the PRO14 competition (now the United Rugby Championship). Players and coaches praised her calm manner and clear decision-making. Hollie believes refereeing is "very mentally and physically demanding. It definitely, mentally, is more draining than playing."

2022 was Hollie's most momentous year so far. She was asked to referee the Sevens World Cup final in the South African city of Cape Town. Two months later, she was in New Zealand to referee the Women's World Cup final between England and the Black Ferns.

Also in 2022, she became the first woman to referee a men's Six Nations team, when she was in charge of Italy's game versus Portugal. Hollie was part of an all-female team of officials, with Sara Cox and Aurélie Groizeleau as her touch judges and Claire Hodnett as the television match official. "I couldn't believe it when I first heard the news," she exclaimed.

"It's pretty cool, and I've been blown away by the responses. It was special to do it with those three, but it was also for everyone who had been grafting for years before us."

Funny Forgetfulness

Sometimes old habits die hard – especially when you're an international superstar.

Legendary All Black George Nēpia played a total of 46 matches for New Zealand. He was venerated as a national treasure in his home country, and admired throughout the world for his skills on the pitch. On the All Blacks tour of the UK in 1924, he was the only player to play in all 32 matches.

After retiring, George continued to take part in charity games. In one match, he saw the ball pop up invitingly from a scrum. He grabbed it and dived over for a try. The only trouble was . . . George was the referee that day. Oops!

Bad-luck Baguette!

IIn 1911, Gaston Vareilles was picked as a winger for France in a Five Nations Championship match against Scotland, to be played in Paris.

On the day of the match, Gaston boarded the team train, heading for the French capital. He was excited. This would be his international debut.

When the train stopped at Lyon, Gaston jumped out. He was peckish and there were a few minutes to spare before the train set off again. He walked down the platform in search of the buffet, in order to buy a baguette for lunch. But – disaster!

– the queue was so long that when he returned to his platform, the train had left without him. Oh, *non*!

Gaston hopped on the next train and made it to Paris just in time for the game. But it was still too late! The manager had picked someone else – an athlete called André Francquenelle, who volunteered to make up the numbers (at the time, teams didn't travel with loads of replacement players).

France won a narrow game 16–15 and Francquenelle did well enough that he was picked twice more for the national team. As for poor Gaston, well, he never played for France again!

The Quadfather

When Duncan Campbell was just 17, he was involved in a diving accident, which resulted in a terrible injury, paralysing him from the waist down.

Duncan lived in Winnipeg, Canada. He had been a sporty teenager before his injury, playing team games like hockey and lacrosse. Now, he vowed to stay active and began hunting down sports, such as table tennis and weight training, that he could take part in with his disability.

The only team sport available at the time was wheelchair basketball. But this required the strength and mobility to be able to throw the ball up into the high basketball hoop – not possible for all wheelchair users.

In 1977, Duncan and four other young men –
Gerry Terwin, Randy Dueck, Paul LeJeune and
Chris Sargent – were at a rehabilitation centre in
Winnipeg. They were expecting to perform some
weight training with the help of a volunteer trainer.
But that day their trainer was a no-show, so the five
of them decided to head to the centre's sports hall to
have a play around.

They found a volleyball, much lighter than a
basketball, and began to pass it around. They also
lined up two rubbish bins at each end of the court to
serve as makeshift hoops or goals. But Duncan and
his friends struggled to get the ball out of the bins
each time they scored. So, they changed the rules:
in order to score, they would have to cross a try line
with the ball in their hands.

In less than an hour, the five players had created the foundations of a whole new sport. They refined the rules over further trips to the sports hall and came up with the name 'Murderball'.

To Duncan's surprise, their new sport caught on. Canada had its first national championships in 1979. That same year, Murderball was first played in the United States.

It wasn't long before Murderball got a name change – to wheelchair rugby – and in 2000, it made its debut as a medal sport at the Sydney Paralympics. Duncan had stayed involved, helping to promote the sport, organising more teams and players to take part. He coached the Canadian team at the 2000 Paralympics and went on to help organise the world championships in 2010. In between, Canada's national championship was renamed the Campbell Cup in his honour. Wow!

Wheelchair rugby is now played in more than 60 nations and is growing all the time. The current men's world champions are Australia, a title previously held by Japan. The current Paralympic gold medallists are Great Britain, and the team with the most titles is the United States. The game is truly worldwide!

Duncan, whose nickname is 'the Quadfather', continues to take part.

"It's fantastic to see so many people playing, watching and enjoying this game . . . that came out of a rehab gym all those years ago. I can't really put it into words."

How to play wheelchair rugby

Four players (out of a squad of 12) are on the pitch at any one time.

The aim is to score by crossing the try line with two wheelchair wheels on the ground and the ball under control. Players can bounce or pass the ball, providing their pass is level or backwards. They can also carry the ball on and between their legs. Players move and block their opponents to create space.

Is wheelchair rugby a contact sport? You betcha! Collisions and tackles are fast and furious and you'll often see players and their chairs knocked over in the impact.

Key rules

Wheelchair rugby has some cool rules to encourage attacking play and all-action games:

• Each team has just 12 seconds to move the ball out of their half of the pitch.

• A player can't hog the ball. They have to pass it within ten seconds.

• The team with the ball has 40 seconds to score, otherwise the ball is handed to their opponents.

History Mystery

Who was the first female rugby player? Sadly we'll never know. We do know that most rugby officials, in the UK and other countries, stopped women and girls from playing for a long, long time. Scandalous!

We also know that the first recorded female rugby player was Emily Valentine. In 1887, Emily was just ten years old and a pupil at Portora Royal School in Enniskillen, Northern Ireland. She loved rugby and her greatest ambition was to score a try. But she wasn't normally allowed to join in:"I used to stand on the touch line in the cold damp Enniskillen winter watching every moment of play."

Then, one day, a team of boys were a player short. After pestering her two brothers, they agreed to let

Emily take part. She took off her hat and coat and joined in. Luckily she always wore boy's boots!

Emily was put out on the wing. Some of the game passed her by until, at last, she had her chance: "I got the ball. I can still feel the damp leather and the smell of it. I grasped it and ran, dodging and darting."

Emily spotted space ahead and raced into it. She kept on going, swerving past an opponent before diving head-first over the line. Try! A cheer rang out from the supporters. Did she enjoy the moment? "It was all I had hoped for," she said.

As far as we know, this game was the start and end of Emily's rugby career. In 1887, there was no chance of a young girl pursuing the sport, even as an amateur. Happily, times have changed!

Lens Me Entertain You

Dolway Walkington played for Ireland eight times between 1887 and 1891, captaining the team twice. He was an attacking full-back who loved to entertain the crowds. But Dolway is best remembered as the only known international to play wearing a monocle (a single glass lens worn over one eye). He would take the monocle off and tuck it into his shorts pocket just before making a tackle!

DID YOU KNOW?

Veterans' rugby is a big deal in Japan with more than 10,000 players in their forties, fifties or older still keeping fit by playing matches. These include second row forward Ryuichi Nagayama who in 2019 turned out for his Fuwaku club at the age of 86!

Diving For Glory

Rugby on land too easy for you? How about playing three to five metres down in a swimming pool!

The brainchild of German diver Ludwig von Bersuda, underwater rugby developed in the 1960s and 1970s. The first European championships took place in the Swedish city of Malmö in 1978, with the first world championships two years later. The 2019 world championships in Austria attracted 18 nations and saw Colombia crowned winners of the men's competition, and Norway, the women's.

The sport is played in a 12m- to 22m-long pool with six players per team, plus loads of subs as the game is very tiring! The players wear masks, snorkels and flippers. The referee wears scuba-diving gear, including an oxygen tank, so they can keep watch without surfacing for air.

The teams must gain the ball, pass and swim with it to place it in metal baskets weighted to the bottom of the pool at each end. The ball is filled with salty water so that it sinks slowly in a freshwater swimming pool. Passes can be forward, backward or to the side, but the ball tends to travel only one or two metres, so the positioning of a team's players is crucial.

Whilst it doesn't look a lot like rugby on land, one thing is common to both sports: ferocious tackling and competing for the ball! No hitting or kicking other players though, or you'll be sent off for two minutes – or permanently. Players can't swim to the surface and throw the ball through the air. All the action – and there's plenty of it – must happen underwater!

North Pole Play

The world's most northerly game of rugby took place at the magnetic North Pole in 2015. One team was led by ex-England sevens captain Ollie Phillips. In charge of their opponents was former England full-back Tim Stimpson. The sevens match was played out on a full-sized pitch marked out on the snow and refereed by a third ex-England player, Lee Mears. Beforehand, the players had had to trek for a week over the ice to reach the pole, some hauling sleds weighing as much as 60kg.

Once they arrived, they had to make the pitch. They had even brought their own goal posts. The players played the match in full cold-weather gear – you would too, in temperatures as low as a teeth-chatteringly bitter -30°C!

> "Having played a lot of rugby up in Newcastle, I've played in some chilly conditions but this was another level altogether!"
>
> – Tim Stimpson

In the end, Team Tim narrowly defeated Team Ollie (17–14) and more than half a million pounds was raised for charity. Brrrrr-illiant!

DID YOU KNOW?

When English team Castleford Tigers were sponsored by a hydraulics and tubing company for the 2014 Super League season, their stadium was renamed the Mend-A-Hose Jungle!

Roo Wouldn't Believe It!

A 2018 women's rugby league match at the Pioneer Oval in Parkes, Australia had to be halted . . . because a kangaroo invaded the pitch. It bounded its way along the full length of the pitch, weaving in and out of players. The two teams, Nyngan and the Spacecats, were only not hopping mad – they thought it was hilarious.

Pants!

Who needs a full kit in order to deliver a great performance . . .

Former Irish rugby union lock Donncha O'Callaghan was playing for Munster against Cardiff in a crucial Heineken Cup match. During play, Donncha's shorts were ripped off him, revealing a pair of bright red underpants. Oops!

As he ran over to the sideline to catch the spare pair of shorts that were thrown to him, the referee called a line-out. Donncha was needed – right now! So he threw the shorts back and joined the line-out just in his pants. He nearly played on shorts-less . . . until the referee insisted he put a pair on!

The Original Billy Whizz

Name: William Boston

Born: Cardiff, UK, 1934

Country: Wales

Clubs: Blackpool Borough, Neath, Pontypridd, Wigan

Position: Wing, centre

Famous for: Rapid rugby league winner and record try scorer

Eighteen-year-old Billy Boston and his mum looked at their kitchen table with astonishment. Spread out across it was £1,500 in notes. In 1953, that was enough to buy you a house. Billy had never seen such a large sum of money before. His mum hadn't either!

So, why was Billy Boston staring at this huge sum of cash? The answer was rugby. Specifically, the Wigan rugby league club, who wanted to sign Billy and had sent officials to his Cardiff home to do just that.

Billy's mum tried to shoo the men away. She had a clever idea ofabout how to get rid of them too. Her son would not sign for Wigan unless they doubled their offer, she told them. Surely, that would get them out of the house quickly . . .

She was wrong. A minute later, the officials upped

their offer to £3,000. It was a phenomenal sum of money, one that they couldn't refuse. Billy became a Wigan player.

It was money well spent. Billy had been a rugby union player, andso, in between games, he had to get to grips with rugby league tactics. "They had me learning how to play the ball in corridors at hotels," he said later. Luckily, he adapted quickly and proved to be a thrillingly brilliant player. He scored an unbelievable 478 tries in 487 matches for Wigan. The fans adored him and raised money to build a statue in the town to commemorate his achievements.

Seeing Red

Don't joke around with a rugby referee during a game, especially if it's a ref who has been in charge of two Rugby World Cup finals.

In a South African match between Griquas and Golden Lions, referee André Watson was telling off a Golden Lions forward when another player, Balie Swart, approached. He had a red card in his hand and brandished it as if he was sending the ref off . . . before handing it to Watson. Ha ha! Good joke!

Unfortunately for Baile, the ref didn't see the funny side – he sent Swart off for his mucking around. Harsh!

Car Trouble

During a tense 1996 Pilkington Cup semi-final game,
London Irish were leading Leicester by just one
point. The ref had called a scrum and the two sets of
forwards were packing down.

Leicester's side included the formidable Martin
Johnson and Dean Richards among its forwards,
whilst Gary Halpin was in the front row for London
Irish. Gary had arrived late for the game in his green
Volvo estate car, rushing to park, change and make
it onto the pitch just in time.

As the scrum packed down in front of thousands
of fans, an announcement came over the stadium
speakers. A car was blocking an exit to the ground

and needed to be moved – immediately. Gary froze
as the announcer gave out the vehicle details.

"That's my car!"

The game was stopped while a red-faced Gary left
the scrum, ran over to the stands and asked his team's
manager to move the car – while the laughing fans
looked on. Oops!

The break didn't help his team. They went on to lose
46–21 to Leicester. "I still get stick for it," Gary
reflected years later. "But some of the penalties I gave
away in my career were way more embarrassing!"

A Real Toothache

In April 2007, Ben Czislowski was playing for the Wynnum rugby league team when he collided with an opponent. The collision gave Ben a wound on his head – but medics stitched it up quickly so that he could carry on playing.

Three months later, though, Ben was still getting headaches. Surely it couldn't be because of the collision? He had even played the rest of that game!

Ben went to the doctors, where he found out the gruesome truth (or should we say . . . tooth). Ben's opponent's tooth was still embedded in his head. Urgh!

Double Trouble

Only two scrum halves have ever won the coveted World Rugby Player of the Year and both are French! In 2002, Fabien Galthié beat other nominees, including legends Jason Robinson, Richie McCaw and Brian O'Driscoll, to win the award.

In 2021, superstar scrum half Antoine Dupont won the award, ahead of England's Maro Itoje and the Australian pair of Samu Kerevi and Michael Hooper. It was well-deserved as Antoine had been on electric form for France, where his head coach was . . . Fabien Galthié!

Selection Error

Have you ever received a message that's changed your life?

In 1906, medical student Arnold Alcock received a letter that filled him with excitement. It was from England's rugby selectors – he had been chosen to play for England against the South African team who were touring the UK.

Arnold was delighted – although a little surprised. He played rugby for Guy's Hospital in London. Playing for his country would be a big step up. But Arnold embraced the challenge. He showed up for the match and put in his best performance.

The trouble was, Arnold's best performance was not

nearly good enough! With this amateur addition to the side, England were lucky to get away with a 3–3 draw! What on earth had gone wrong?

The answer turned out to be simple. The selectors had written to the wrong rugby player. They had meant to select towering Lancashire forward Lancelot Slocock!

Lancelot cursed his luck – while Arnold nursed his pride. But Lancelot got his chance to make his England debut the following year, scoring a try and powering England to a thumping victory, 41–13. Alcock, for his part, completed his studies, became a doctor, and was president of Gloucester Rugby Club from 1924 all the way to 1969. Impressive!

Lucky Charm

Name: Zoe Aldcroft

Born: Scarborough, UK, 1996

Country: England

Clubs: Darlington Mowden Park Sharks, Gloucester-Hartpury Women

Position: Lock

Famous for: Being an elite rugby union second row forward

Many sportspeople have superstitions. English forward Zoe Aldcroft certainly has. If she puts an item of clothing on the wrong way, like a jumper on back to front, she has to stick with it all day. And if she sees a magpie on its own, she will always salute it for luck.

But Zoe's most important good-luck charm is a little woollen doll version of England legend Jonny Wilkinson. It was knitted by a friend's grandmother for teenage Zoe to take with her when she left home to go to Hartpury College in Gloucester.

Nowadays, her little woolly Wilko is always at the bottom of her kit bag, wherever she plays. "The kit is always different. The changing room is always different. The team is always different, but having this one consistent thing helps me relax."

And it certainly hasn't done her any harm. Brilliant in line-outs, Zoe has played more than 30 times for England and appeared in the final of a Rugby World Cup. In December 2021, she was crowned World Rugby's Women's Player of the Year. Woolly well done, Zoe!

Mud, Mud, Glorious Mud

Wales's ground, Cardiff Arms Park, was much loved
by fans. Some 40,000 spectators regularly crammed
inside. But the ground was located on low land near
the River Taff, which sometimes flooded – and this
could lead to some very muddy games!

In 1957, Wales welcomed Ireland to their famous
ground. On the day of the game, the rain fell heavily.
The pitch was soaked through and it didn't take long
for the players to be caked in thick mud, covering
their shirts, shorts – and faces. This made the job of
working out who was playing for which side almost
impossible for referee Jack Taylor.

Early in the second half, Taylor had had enough.
He ordered the Welsh team off the pitch to go and

put on a clean set of shirts, socks and shorts. A sensible solution, which allowed the game to continue and Wales to squeak home winners, 6–5.

But not everyone saw it that way. Rather than being praised for his actions, Taylor was told off – and he wasn't given another international match to referee for three years! His first game back? Wales versus South Africa at Cardiff Arms Park. This match was even muddier, and not long afterwards, further rain flooded the pitch. It was completely underwater!

DID YOU KNOW?

One of the soggiest games on record was between Scotland and New Zealand, at Eden Park, Auckland, in 1975. Nicknamed The Waterpolo Test, the match would probably have been postponed if Scotland hadn't been due to fly home the next day!

Scrum Numbers

Scrum time is when a team's forwards bend low and strain every sinew to do battle as a unit with their opponents. In rugby union, all eight forwards pack down for a scrum with the ball fed down the middle by the scrum half.

Scrums can be ferocious tests of raw power. In a 2017 English National League match between Hinckley and Luctonians, Hinckley's scrum drove their opponents back so hard into the goal posts that the posts collapsed and toppled over! Luckily, no one was hurt and there was a spare pitch to continue the game.

In rugby league, six players from each side form a scrum, whilst scrums in sevens are just three-a-side.

Imagine a rugby scrum with not three, six or eight but 879 players per side! It happened in New Zealand in 2017 . . .

Kids from a high school in Palmerston provided some of the players but in the end, the whole town took part.

"The whole community dug in, which made it very special – I'm really chuffed."
– Karen Heaphy, organiser

New Zealand rugby star Selica Winiata was given the special task of putting the ball into the super-sized scrum!

Schoolboy Success

On their 1935 tour of Great Britain, New Zealand had managed to lose just once in 67 matches by the time they faced Swansea at St Helen's on 28th September.

Swansea's attacks were led by Willie Davies and Haydn Tanner, who were still pupils at Gowerton County School. The pair were cousins and had a brilliant game, constantly finding spaces in the All Blacks defence and keeping their opponents' attacks in check. Swansea ran out famous 11–3 winners.

All Blacks captain Jack Manchester congratulated Swansea, saying, "Hadyn Tanner and Willie Davies gave a wonderful performance." But he begged reporters: "Please don't tell them back home in New Zealand we were beaten by a pair of schoolboys!"

An Astonishing Comeback

Name: Ian McKinley

Born: Dublin, Ireland, 1989

Country: Ireland

Clubs: Benetton Treviso, Leinster, Leonorso Udine, Viadana, Zebre

Position: Fly half

Famous for: Fly half who made a stirring comeback from a seemingly career-ending injury

In 2010, aged 19, Ian McKinley was a promising rugby union fly half, playing for the University College Dublin team. He had already played for top Irish club, Leinster, and had a glittering future ahead of him. That crumbled in the fraction of a second it took an accidental boot to strike his face.

In the accident, Ian lost the sight in his left eye. He had barely begun his rugby career when he was forced to retire. He moved to Udine in Italy to begin rugby coaching and a little later got the chance to work with Raleri, an Italian ski-goggle manufacturer. Together with his brother, Philip, and a design student called Johnny Merrigan, Ian helped to perfect a pair of plastic rugby goggles that would protect his one good eye and be safe for opponents coming into contact with him. Now, Ian could think about returning to the pitch . . .

So, three years after he had retired, Ian started all over again. He had to work hard to regain his skills and sharpness. Having only one eye made judging distances harder and he had to alter his kicking and passing technique to allow for his visual impairment. Eventually, though, in 2014, he played his first game back – his debut for Leonorso, a third division Italian team.

"It was raining, muddy. We won 65–5 and it was a great feeling."

– Ian McKinley

Once again, Ian's talent shone – so much so that he was soon snapped up by higher-ranked Italian clubs, first Zebre and then, in 2016, Benetton Treviso, winners of 15 Italian national championships.

Ian had been living in Italy for more than five years

when a stunning invitation reached him. He had been selected for the Italian national team. He came off the replacements bench to make his debut against Fiji in 2017, and scored the last points of the game as Italy ran out 19–10 winners.

Ian played a further eight times for Italy, his last match – against Ireland – taking place in his home town of Dublin. And the eyewear that Ian pioneered has gone on to help many other players with eye problems prolong their careers, including All Blacks legend Ardie Savea. Ian celebrated his achievement in a 2020 interview:

"**Knowing that 2,000 people around the world are using rugby goggles is wonderful.**"

Ian, we agree!

Fabulous Fiji

Rugby was played at four early Olympics. The 1924 competition was its last, mostly because only three teams turned up – the United States, France and Romania. Romania won the bronze medal despite heavily losing both their matches. Campaigners tried to get rugby back into the games for decades without luck, until sevens events for men's and women's teams were introduced to the 2016 Olympics in Rio de Janeiro, Brazil. Sevens were a roaring success at the games, partly due to the incredible story of the men's gold medallists – the amazing team from Fiji.

This small island nation had been through devastating tropical storms earlier that year, with many villages destroyed. Some of the players had lost friends or family members to the disaster. The rugby team had little funding compared to other sides. In the years before the Olympics, their coach, Ben Ryan, had to beg and borrow to get accommodation, training kit and pitch time.

Despite these obstacles, the flying Fijians were ranked number one in the world. But could they bring home Fiji's first Olympic medal? The nation had never won gold in any sport.

Work and school on the island pretty much stopped during the 2016 tournament. The whole of Fiji was glued to TV screens, willing their side on. They topped their group, winning all three games, but then came the big test, New Zealand, in the quarter finals.

Fiji snuck through 12–7. Next they defeated Japan in the semis, to face Great Britain – their coach

Ben Ryan's home nation – in the final.

Fiji played a devastating and wildly entertaining match with delicate passes, out-of-this-world offloads and amazing pace and power. They scored seven tries and were far too much for the GB team, who lost 43–7.

Fiji had finally won an Olympic medal – a GOLD one – and it was in the nation's favourite sport. Back home, the celebrations had begun, and they reached a frenzy when the tired but triumphant team returned. A national holiday was declared for the following day and the players and coach found their faces on Fiji's money – a brand-new seven-dollar banknote commemorating their win!

Four years later – well, five actually, after the 2020 Olympics was delayed for a year due to the

COVID-19 pandemic – it was joy once more for Fiji. The men won gold again, whilst the rapidly improving women's team, the Fijiana, beat Great Britain to win a bronze medal. Super sevens all round!

"I feel very lucky I am in charge of such an unbelievable group of athletes with a country behind us that is so passionate about rugby sevens."

– Ben Ryan, Fiji coach

Old Hands

On 26th August 2006, Dennis Gleeson turned out for the State Rail Apprentice Rugby League Club in Australia. Wearing the number 12 jersey, Dennis was playing in the New South Wales Tertiary Student League. There was nothing unusual in that – except that Dennis was 70 years and nine days old. He is the oldest rugby league player on record!

The oldest international rugby union player was Mark Spencer, who played for Qatar versus Uzbekistan in the Asian Five Nations competition (now called the Asia Rugby Championship). He was 57 years and 340 days old.

Rapid Red

Rugby league 'Ashes' matches between Great Britain and Australia are often very physical battles. None more so than in a 2003 game at Wigan. GB's Sean Long kicked the ball high and deep into the Australian half. It was caught by Robbie Kearns, who was immediately flattened by GB forward Adrian Morley.

Apart from being the first tackle of the game, it was high and against the rules. The referee, Steve Ganson, showed Morley the red card and he had to leave the field after just 12 seconds of play. Oops!

Young Lion

Name: Oghenemaro Miles Itoje (Maro)

Born: Camden, London, 1994

Country: England

Clubs: Saracens

Position: Lock, blindside flanker

Famous for: A rugby union superstar, whose exceptional defensive skills, line-out abilities and leadership have wowed the rugby world

Oghenemaro Miles Itoje, better known as Maro, is one of the world's best locks. These players need to be towering jumpers at line-outs and under the high ball, add power in the scrum and rampage around the field, making carries and tackles. Maro is one of the best at all facets of the game.

He's proven to be an inspirational force, whether playing for his club, Saracens, or for England in the second row (or occasionally as a flanker in the back row).

From May 2015 to September 2016, Maro played in 31 competitive matches for these two sides . . . and didn't lose one. During that time, Saracens became back-to-back English Premiership and European champions.

The following year, he was selected for the 2017 British & Irish Lions – a great honour. Rarely has a player with just 12 caps for his country made the squad, let alone played in the actual Test matches.

Despite being the youngest player on the tour, the 22 year old formed a formidable second-row partnership with Welsh veteran Alun Wyn Jones. Maro played in all three Tests against the mighty All Blacks, winning one, losing one, and drawing the final match and series overall. In more than a century of tours, it was only the second time the Lions had not lost a series in New Zealand!

"Being part of the Lions is a bit like cheesecake . . . you have one taste, then you want another."

– Maro Itoje

Maro was back four years later as the Lions toured South Africa, who were defending world champions. The Lions suffered a painful 19–16 defeat in the third Test to narrowly lose the series. Maro, though, was voted Player of the Series by his Lions team-mates.

Providing he keeps his great form and steers clear of injury, Maro is likely to make his third tour to Australia in 2025. He's unlikely to match the Irish legend Willie John McBride though. Willie went on five Lions tours as a player and a sixth as manager!

Maro was back four years later as the Lions toured South Africa who were defending world champions. The Lions suffered a painfully 19–16 defeat in the Third Test to narrowly lose the series. Maro, though, was voted the Lions' Player of the Series by his teammates.

Providing he keeps his great form and steers clear of injury, Maro is likely to make his third tour in 2025 to Australia. He's unlikely to match the Irish legend, Willie John McBride though. He went on five Lions tours as a player and a sixth as manager!

WHO ARE THE LIONS?

Once every four years, England, Ireland, Wales and Scotland join together to send a combined elite team on tour. Their destination is one of the three southern hemisphere rugby powerhouses: Australia, New Zealand or South Africa.

The Lions play warm-up matches against regional or select sides before competing in three intense Test matches against the home nation. For most British or Irish rugby players, being selected for the Lions is the pinnacle of their career.

Through the Posts!

A drop goal in rugby is a kick from the hand aimed at goal. If it sails through the posts, then your team are in the points. In rugby league, a drop goal is only worth one point, but in union, it's worth three times as much (before 1948, drop goals were worth four points).

Drop goals can be taken from anywhere on the pitch. In 1932, South African Gerry Brand struck an ENORMOUS 77.7m-long drop goal against England. Another South African holds the record for the most drop goals in an international game: Jannie de Beer struck five in just 18 minutes to knock England out of the 1999 Rugby World Cup. Wow!

Don't fret for England though. At the next World Cup, a drop goal from Jonny Wilkinson made them the first

World Cup winners from Europe. Jonny ended his career with 36 drop goals for England, the most of any international player.

A drop goal mustn't hit the ground before going through the posts – but it can hit a player on the way.

In a 2001 Heineken Cup game, Gloucester were losing 25–27 to Llanelli with seconds to go on the clock. The ball came back to Gloucester scrum half Elton Moncrieff right in front of the posts. He had little choice but to have a go – and hit the ball terribly. It flew just a metre above the ground, but bounced off a Llanelli forward and looped up and over the bar. Three points and a Gloucester win!

DID YOU KNOW?

In 2020, whilst playing for the Hurricanes, New Zealand back Jordie Barrett struck a 63m-long penalty from well inside his own half between the goal posts. It's the longest known place kick in Super Rugby (a club competition featuring Australia, Fiji, New Zealand and the Pacific Islands).

Foggy Fun

England's men's rugby union team were battling with Wales in a 1908 match at Bristol. There was a problem though . . . The whole ground was covered in thick, thick fog, making it impossible to see one side of the pitch from the other!

Wales's full-back Bert Winfield kicked three goals, doing well to work out where the posts were. Some of the players could only hear their team-mates, not see them. It can't have been much fun for the spectators! Today, the referee would call off a game in those conditions – but back then, the players pressed on and the game ended up in a 28–18 victory for Wales.

But the funniest moment took place after the game . . .

Once the Welsh players were back in their dressing room, they realised they were one short. Their full-back, Bert Winfield, was missing. Bert was still out on the pitch, staring into the fog, unaware that the game was over!

Rugby has always been a sport played in all weathers but, sometimes, it gets a bit silly. The mighty All Blacks faced a midweek game against Welsh club Llanelli in 1989. Llanelli was not the only opponent they faced – a powerful, stormy wind was whipping across the pitch. When the All Blacks' famous fly half Grant Fox tried to take a drop-out kick, the wind blew the ball way back over his head. Somehow, the All Blacks still managed to win, 11–0!

Awesome All-Rounder

Canadian legend Heather Moyse played at two Rugby World Cups, 2006 and 2010. At both, she was sole or joint leading try scorer. She was the leading scorer at the 2008 Hong Kong Sevens. But a stellar rugby career was just part of Heather's sporting success story —she was also a sprinter and a triple-jump champion, and she played football and won two Winter Olympic gold medals in bobsleigh, hurtling down an icy track. Phew!

As if that wasn't enough, in 2012, she represented Canada in track-cycling. What an incredible all-rounder!

Trailblazers

Women's rugby league in Great Britain in the 1980s and 90s was a Cinderella sport. It was enjoyed passionately by its players, but you never saw it on TV or read about it in the newspapers. Most of the public were unaware that women even played the sport – and played it well.

In 1994, an invite to tour in Australia reached rugby league coach Jackie Sheldon. She and a group of players, including Lisa McIntosh and Brenda Dobek, formed a GB committee. A lot had to be organised and there was little help or funding from the men's game.

The players, who were amateurs, had to raise a lot of money to be able to fly out and stay in Australia. Some spent their savings. Some were sponsored by councils or companies, and some borrowed from friends and family. The players also held bucket collections at games, sold stuff at car boot sales and did sponsored walks to raise money.

The British Lionesses flew out in the summer of 1996. No British women's rugby league team had toured abroad before. The players didn't know what to expect in Australia. It was a genuine trip into the unknown.

> **"We just went to give a good account and not show ourselves up."**
> – Lisa McIntosh, captain of the Lionesses

There were a few hiccups when they arrived. The coach that greeted them at the airport wasn't big enough to carry all the players and their bags. The white shorts of their kit turned out to be see-through – new ones had to be bought from a local sports shop! But they were heartened by the welcome they received. Several major men's clubs, including the Brisbane Broncos, donated kit and invited the Lionesses to train with them.

On the pitch, the Lionesses hit the ground running. They enjoyed two walloping warm-up wins, including an 86–0 triumph against a Sydney Select XIII.

Next they faced Australia.

The first Test was a tightly fought game, with Australia winning narrowly, 16–14. Despite nursing injuries, the Lionesses roared back in the second Test, scoring four tries to win 18–12. How would the final game play out? It would be hard to call . . .

The final game was just as tight as the first – but the Lionesses did it! They won 20–18. They had secured the series!

"I don't think we could ask for a better Test series," said Australian captain Julie McGuffie afterwards. "Each game went right down to the wire and we were beaten by a very good team."

There was no parade or crowds to greet the triumphant Lionesses when they returned home. But positive changes to women's rugby league did start to happen, albeit slowly. They toured New Zealand in 1998, and in 2000, their coach Jackie Sheldon was asked to help organise a Women's Rugby League World Cup. Slowly, slowly, the women's game grew – all thanks to the tenacious, trailblazing Lionessses and their Ashes tour.

> ## "It was the start of something and it's really grown into something special."
> – Brenda Dobek

Try . . . Faster!

The fastest try ever scored at a Rugby World Cup was scored by Australia's Elton Flatley versus Romania in 2003. Elton had started the game with a kick. The Australian forwards won the ball, passed it to Elton, who powered over the line, all in 18 seconds.

But Elton's try was snail's pace compared with the fastest try of all . . .

This was scored in an English National League 1 game between Doncaster Knights and Old Albanians in 2013. Doncaster Knights kicked off with a toweringly high kick. The ball landed and bounced over the heads of some Old Albanians players, straight into the hands of Doncaster Knights winger Tyson Lewis. He raced over to score a try timed at just 7.24 seconds. Rapid!

Three Nations

Rugby union players sometimes change positions once or twice throughout their careers. Jonah Lomu, for example, began as a forward in the back row before becoming a powerful winger. But few players swapped positions – or countries – as much as Enrique Edgardo Rodríguez.

Aged 19, Enrique began as a winger for the National University of Córdoba Rugby Club. He moved to centre, then fly half, then into the forwards in the back row, before finally becoming a skilful prop forward in the front row.

Enrique made his debut for Argentina in 1979 versus New Zealand, and played 13 times for his country. His last match for the Pumas was in Australia in 1983.

Enrique liked Australia so much that, seven months later, he moved there, and in 1984 began a run of 26 matches for Australia. In 1981, he also played a match for Tahiti, making Enrique the only known rugby union player to have played for three different countries. Amazing!

DID YOU KNOW?

The 2023 men's and women's Six Nations saw the debut of Sportable's smart ball. It handles like a normal rugby ball but contains sensors that allow its position to be tracked 20 times a second. This allows stattos to compile all sorts of facts and figures, from how long the ball spends in the air to the longest kicks and fastest ball carriers. Wow!

Sevens Heaven

In its early days, rugby could be chaotic. Initially each side was made up of 30 or more players. In 1847, new rules fixed the precise number of players on the pitch. The figure 20 was chosen: three full-backs and 17 forwards per team. Unlike in modern rugby, though, the players didn't really work together. They charged around and did their own thing!

Hely Hutchinson Almond, the headmaster of the Loretto School in Scotland, thought this was a shame. He started organising matches between teams with fewer people, to encourage the players to find space and pass to their team-mates. Almond ran various 11-a-side rugby games, and in 1871, he was one of the umpires at the very first rugby international: Scotland versus England.

Twelve years later, in 1893, another experiment changed the sport. This time, it was the brainchild of a local butcher called Ned Haig. Ned's team, Melrose Rugby Club, also in Scotland, had hit hard times and he came up with the idea of a fund-raising sports day featuring a rugby tournament. Each game would be 15 minutes long and feature seven-a-side teams. As Ned said, "It was hopeless to think of having several games in one afternoon with 15 players on each side."

Some people laughed. Others wondered how a game with so few people could be played on a full-sized rugby pitch. They needn't have worried. The tournament attracted seven teams – Selkirk, St Cuthbert's Hawick, Earlston, Gala Forest, St Ronan's Innerleithen, Gala and Melrose – and a crowd of thousands. More than 1,600 spectators came via special trains laid on for the event. It was a roaring success!

Melrose won the competition and their captain David Sanderson was awarded the Ladies Cup – a small silver goblet donated by the ladies of the town – for the tournament's best player. Sanderson was Ned Haig's boss at the butchers!

The seven-a-side game – or 'sevens' – spread throughout the borders region of Scotland and, over the decades, further afield. The famous Middlesex Sevens kicked off in 1926, and exactly 50 years later, the Hong Kong Sevens began. In 2016, rugby sevens became a new sport at the Olympics, and proved a hit with spectators. Australia won gold in the first women's competition, whilst Fiji triumphed in the men's (see page 78). Meanwhile, back in Scotland, the Melrose Sevens is still held every year at Greenyards, the ground where Ned's original sevens competition was played.

Oh, Brother!

When Slovenia played Bulgaria in 2014, there was a lot of brotherly love on the pitch . . .

The Slovenian team started with three brothers, Archie, Frank and George Skofic, who all played the full 80 minutes. After 25 minutes, the trio were joined by their brother Max. He made up for lost time by scoring three tries. George also scored a try and Frank scored two points by kicking a conversion.

In the 77th minute, the four brothers became five when Jack came on as a late replacement – the only time five brothers (or sisters) have played rugby together for a national team. What's more, Slovenia triumphed, winning 43–17. Awesome!

Pacific Powerhouse

In 1924, the Fijian rugby team left their island to play an international match for the very first time. The entire cost of the tour – £160 (almost £8,000 in today's money) – had been raised by local people.

The players climbed aboard a steamship, the MV *Tofua*, which cruised its way 1,100km across the Pacific to reach Apia, the capital of Samoa. The very next day, at seven in the morning, Fiji's match kicked off. They were starting early so that the Samoan players could go to work afterwards! And this wasn't the only unusual thing about the match. Fiji played in all-black strips whilst Samoa played in all-white. Both teams played barefoot, kicking the ball with no protection. Ouch! They also had to avoid the tree that grew out of the middle of the pitch, near the halfway line!

Samoa's forwards were huge and strong and threatened to overpower the Fijians. But superior passing and jinking skills saw Fiji score two tries, the first by winger Viliame Devo, the second by centre Savenaca Tamanibeka. The small crowd of 500 or 600 people were impressed by the Fijians' speed and agility as they ran out 6–0 winners.

The Samoan Times newspaper failed to cover the historic match. Why? Because their rugby reporter was watching a game of hopscotch instead! The newspaper later issued an apology.

As for the Fijians, after the game, they re-boarded their steamship, which sailed on another 900km to Tonga. There, they won seven and drew one of the nine matches they played, proving themselves a mighty rugby force in the Pacific.

Perfect Portia

Only a handful of top players can ever become top try scorer at a Rugby World Cup. New Zealand star Portia Woodman has managed it twice, in 2017 and 2022. Epic!

In 2022, whilst playing against Canada, Portia also became the first woman to score 200 tries in the World Rugby Women's Sevens Series. In fact, her team-mates had been so confident that she would score that they had already printed special T-shirts congratulating her!

Mascot Mayhem

Some rugby league teams have mascots dressed up in costumes to rouse the crowd and entertain fans at games. In the Australian National Rugby League (NRL), these range from Victor the Viking (Canberra Raiders) and Timmy the Tiger (Wests Tigers) to MC Hammerhead (Cronulla-Sutherland Sharks).

In 1995, Stanley the Steel Avenger from Australia's Illawarra Steelers shocked fans when he ran onto the pitch and began brawling with some of the players. He became the only NRL mascot ever to be shown the red card!

Getting Shirty

Andrew 'Jock' Wemyss was a prop forward who made his debut for Scotland's rugby union team in 1914, shortly before World War I broke out. Jock lost an eye in battle but resumed playing rugby after the war ended in 1918.

In 1920, he was selected for Scotland's first peacetime match against France. He turned up at the ground with his Edinburgh rugby shorts and socks, and waited patiently to be given a Scotland shirt.

Jock waited and waited . . . but no Scottish jersey came. When he asked what the problem was, the Scotland selector got (ahem!) shirty with him. He said that Jock was supposed to bring his Scotland shirt from six years earlier. But Jock had swapped shirts with an opponent that day. What's more, Jock pointed out angrily, there had been the small matter of a world war in between games!

Still . . . no shirt was offered.

With the game due to start, the team lined up to head onto the pitch. Jock, bare-chested, joined the other players. But in 1920, to head out into the stadium half-naked was unthinkable! Suddenly, just in time, a shirt was found for him – and Jock enjoyed a 5–0 win over France.

During the game, he found that his opposite number in the scrum, Toulouse forward Marcel-Frédéric Lubin-Lebrère, had also lost an eye during the war. The pair went on to become lifelong friends.

Just in Time

It was a Saturday in January 1930, around midday, when Sam Tucker got an urgent phone call. It was from the English RFU (Rugby Football Union) secretary. "Get to Cardiff quickly. You're playing in the match this afternoon."

The game was Wales versus England, and a late injury to forward Henry Rew meant that Sam was suddenly needed. Gulp!

Sam was in Bristol and there was little more than an hour before kick-off. The only way to get to Cardiff in time was by plane! Sam had never flown before. After a short but harrowing flight in a two-seater biplane, he landed in a field close to Cardiff Arms Park. From there, he hitched a lift on a passing coal lorry. When he finally got to the ground, he had to convince officials at the stadium to let him in!

Just FIVE MINUTES before kick-off, Sam burst into the England changing room. He made it out onto the field just in time . . . and played a storming game as England won 11 – 3. He ended up playing for England for the rest of the Five Nations competition. Super Sam!

DID YOU KNOW?

Legendary Welsh referee Nigel Owens has taken charge of more international rugby matches than any other official – 100 matches in all. He's also refereed 149 PRO14 games, 98 Heineken or European Champions Cup games and the 2015 Rugby World Cup final.

Man Versus Cheetah
(Versus Plane)

Name: Bryan Habana

Born: Johannesburg, South Africa, 1983

Country: South Africa

Clubs: Blue Bulls, Bulls, Golden Lions, Stormers, Toulon, Western Province

Position: Winger

Famous for: Lightning-fast winger and try scorer

These days, Bryan Habana is known as a rugby commentator and businessman, but as a player, he was a skilful and super-speedy winger – the fastest top player in the game. A World Cup winner with South Africa in 2007, Bryan finished his career with 67 tries for his country – the second highest tally of all time, behind Japan's Daisuke Ohata's 69 tries.

In 2007, at the peak of his playing career, Bryan was invited to take part in a challenge: racing a two-and-a-half-year-old cheetah called Cetane. The 100m race was to help raise awareness of the threats faced by big cats in Africa. Cheetahs are the world's fastest land animal, reaching speeds of up to 120kmph. Would Bryan stand a chance? Not really! Even with a 30m head start, he was powerless to stop Cetane whizz past!

Six years later, Bryan was pitted against a very different speed machine – a brand-new Airbus A380 airliner. The contest took place along a 100m stretch of runway at Manston Airport in Kent. This time, the result was different. Despite the airliner's four powerful jet engines, Bryan won with ease!

Day Jobs

In the past, few players got the chance to play professionally. Most had to work day jobs to support their career in rugby.

Scotland and Harlequins full-back Chloe Rollie worked as a dump-truck driver, whilst current England front rower Hannah Botterman was a painter and decorator, and Shaunagh Brown was a firefighter. Possibly the coolest day job was held by England's star winger from the 1990s, Rory Underwood. Rapid Rory is still England's record try scorer with 49 international tries, but off the pitch, he went even faster – as a jet-fighter pilot in the RAF!

You Can't Be Serious, Ref!

In 2015, a charity match was held between the England Legends, including former England captain Martin Corry, and an Irish Legends team, which included former players Mick Galwey and Paddy Johns.

The match referee was Alain Rolland, who had refereed the final of the 2007 Rugby World Cup and dozens of other major matches. Alain had played a lot of rugby himself, as a scrum half for Irish side Leinster. He had even won three caps for Ireland in the 1990s. So, knowing the match was for fun, when a scrum formed near the England Legends try line, he couldn't resist . . .

Alain reached down at the back of the English side of the scrum and picked up the ball. He darted over

the line, dived and touched the ball down in front
of startled England players. Then he got up . . . and
made a ref's signal.

TRY!

The Irish cheered. Even the England players saw the
funny side . . . especially as they ran out winners,
58–34, and the match raised thousands of pounds.
Legends!

DID YOU KNOW?

Germany won a silver medal in rugby
union at the 1900 Olympics in Paris despite
losing the only game they played (versus
France). Their second match, against Great
Britain, didn't take place because the GB
team had boat tickets to head home!

Unstoppable Caitlin

Name: Caitlin Beevers

Born: Dewsbury, UK, 2001

Country: England

Clubs: Dewsbury Moor, Leeds Rhinos

Position: Full-back, wing, centre

Famous for: Combining refereeing with a successful playing career

Caitlin Beevers is a woman in a hurry. It isn't just that she's a pacy player; she's crammed a whole career's worth of highlights into just a handful of years as a talented teen rugby league player.

Caitlin started playing rugby league with boys' teams when she was just six. By the age of 12, she was no longer allowed to play with the boys, but couldn't find a suitable girls' team in her local area of West Yorkshire. So, she took up refereeing. A little later, when an opportunity came up to join a girls' rugby side at her new school, Caitlin grabbed the chance. Her school reached the final of the National Schools competition in 2017. Caitlin powered her team to glory, kicking nine goals and scoring five tries – an incredible total of 38 points. She achieved all this while keeping up her referee training.

The following year, 2018, was an even bigger one for Caitlin. She joined top rugby league side Leeds Rhinos, scoring 17 tries in 14 games and winning the 2018 Women's Challenge Cup and the Young Player of the Year. She also played her first match for the England rugby league team, scoring two tries versus France. And that's not all . . .

Imagine walking out onto Wembley Stadium's famous pitch as the referee, to start and control a match with thousands of eyes all on you. Well, at just 17, that's what Caitlin did. She was put in charge of the Champion Schools Final, the game traditionally played before the Men's Challenge Cup Final. Caitlin rose to the occasion, while making history as the first female rugby referee at Wembley Stadium.

"It was one of the best days of my life, it feels absolutely unreal!"

Sadly there isn't much money in women's rugby league in England and players tend to be amateurs. So busy bee Caitlin took a job working in a paint factory. Alongside her twin brother, Josh, she hits the gym two nights a week and trains two nights a week with Leeds Rhinos. She also spends one night a week with other rugby officials, improving her refereeing skills.

And then there's joining up with the rest of the England squad for training and matches . . . Phew! Luckily Caitlin loves her packed life. "It's full on but I've got the best of both worlds. The full-time referees help a lot and I would love to go full-time eventually . . . refereeing massively contributes to my playing."

On the Whistle

Do you know which country is reigning Olympic champion at 15-a-side rugby? Or which country had the first player to be sent off in an international rugby match? Do you know who was referee in the very first Rugby World Cup match in 1987? And can you guess which small item links all three events?

The answer is – wait for it – a referee's whistle!

In the 1880s, Joseph Hudson owned a small metal tool-making company in Birmingham. In 1884, he invented a new type of piercingly loud metal whistle. He named it the Acme Thunderer and its first customers were London's Metropolitan Police force. Soon, new team sports, such as football and rugby, also got interested, buying Thunderers for their officials. A blast on the new whistle could not be ignored!

In 1905, Welsh referee Gil Evans was put in charge of the New Zealand All Blacks' first ever Test match against England. The game was held at Crystal Palace in London, and Evans was given a shiny new Thunderer whistle made of sterling silver.

After the match, Evans generously passed the whistle to another referee, called Albert Freethy. Freethy got the chance to use it in the final game of the 1924 Olympics in Paris. In that match, the United States beat France 17–3 to win the gold medal. As it was the last time regular 15-a-side rugby union appeared at the Olympics, the United States are still Olympic champions.

The following year, 1925, a mighty New Zealand team were near the end of a long tour of Britain. They had played 27 matches and won all of them. That's how good they were! In their 28th game, they faced England in front of a crowd of 60,000. The referee was Albert Freethy and he was kept busy. Fists were flying. There were nasty tackles and barging off the ball. Freethy warned both sides several times in the first five minutes.

But with just eight minutes gone, the ref spied something that deserved more than a warning. Freethy saw All Black forward Cyril Brownlie stamp on an England player's leg. Enough was enough. The ref blew his silver Thunderer whistle to stop the game and sent Brownlie off the pitch. The crowd was stunned into silence. No player in an international game had ever been sent off before. New Zealand eventually won the game – but Brownlie felt terrible. It was an epic 42 years before another player was sent off in an international match.

The famous whistle is now part of rugby folklore. It was donated to the New Zealand Rugby Museum in 1969. Eighteen years later, it was taken out of its case, dusted down and handed to Bob Fordham, the referee in the first match of the first ever Rugby World Cup, in which New Zealand beat Italy by a thumping 70–6.

This began a tradition continued ever since – the silver 'Gil Evans whistle' is blown in the first game of every Rugby World Cup tournament. **Peeeeeeep!**

A Brilliant Bounce-Back

Name: Stephen Crichton

Born: Apia, Samoa, 2000

Country: Samoa

Clubs: Canterbury-Bankstown Bulldogs, New South Wales, Penrith Panthers

Position: Centre, wing, full-back

Famous for: A winning combination of speed, strength and superb finishing skills make him an impressive try scorer

The 2021 Rugby League World Cup (held in 2022) showcased superb skills from the world's top players. It also featured some incredible team performances, including a brave comeback by Toa Samoa – the Samoan's men's side.

Samoa had been placed in the same group as World Cup hosts England. Cheered on by a passionate home crowd, England thrashed them 60–6. To make the day worse, Samoa lost three players to serious injuries. "They outclassed us today," admitted Samoa's captain, Junior Paulo. "But it's the start of the tournament. We've got to go back, regroup and move on to next week. It's a good test of our character, but I still believe we've got a good side here."

Junior was right. Samoa won their next two group games easily and found themselves up against Pacific neighbours Tonga in the quarter finals.

Having defeated Tonga, in the semi-finals they then faced England again. Gulp!

Samoa seized their chance from kick-off, scoring the game's first try and leading 10–6 at half time. In an entertaining match, England hit back, going ahead before Samoa scored again. The game was seesawing wildly, and the 40,000-strong crowd at Emirates Stadium in London were enthralled.

Samoa scored a sensational, high-speed try on the 49th minute. It began with a mazy run by star player Jarome Luai. He passed to captain Junior Paulo, who was tackled but managed to flick the ball skilfully away, back to Jarome, who patted it on to Stephen Crichton to score. Incredible!

But there was barely time to catch their breath before England started pounding the Samoan defence. By the 68th minute, the scores were level. Five minutes later, Samoa thought they had the game won. Their brilliant goal kicker, Stephen Crichton, intercepted an England pass and scored his second try of the night, adding the two points himself. But England roared back, making ground as Samoan legs tired. They got to within five metres of the Samoan try line but could not make it over. There was still five minutes to go . . . then four . . . then three . . .

Time was running out now. But ferocious forward Herbie Farnworth powered over in the 77th minute for an England try. Tommy Makinson then scored the conversion that levelled the scores: 26–26. Moments later, the hooter sounded and the game headed into nerve-wracking extra time. This featured the golden point rule: whoever scored next – try, penalty or drop goal – would win.

Despite seeing victory snatched from them, the Samoans refused to buckle. They repelled an England attack, then ran the ball down the middle of the pitch. It reached Anthony Milford, who tried to score a drop goal, but his kick was charged down. Brutal!

Samoa went again, but this time the ball was passed to Stephen Crichton. Could he hold his nerve and score the golden point?

> **"Stephen Crichton is a history maker! Samoa into the final of the Rugby League World Cup. What a moment for rugby league. What a moment for that nation."**
>
> – Dave Woods, commentator

Stephen and Samoa had done it! The celebrations raged on all night. It was the first time in 16 Rugby League World Cups that a team other than Australia, New Zealand, GB or England had reached the final. "This is what we strive for, to put our little country on the map," said Stephen Crichton after the game. His team-mate, Jarome Luai, who was made Player of the Match added, "I don't think anyone gave us a chance tonight but the belief in the squad is very strong."

A Lotta Line-outs

Line-outs are the way a game of rugby union is restarted after the ball has gone out of the side of the pitch. A dozen or more line-outs in a game is common, but a 1963 Scotland versus Wales match took this to the extreme.

Welsh captain Clive Rowlands decided to keep the ball amongst his forwards. So, whenever he got the ball, he didn't pass to his backs. Instead, he kicked the ball out over the sideline to force a line-out. Wales spent much of the game inside the Scottish half and won 6–0, but spectators were unimpressed – watching 111 line-outs in a single match wasn't the exciting, attacking play they had been hoping for!

All-Rounder Rudie

Rudie van Vuuren is a force to be reckoned with –
and not just on the rugby pitch. He has played a total
of 15 matches for Namibia . . . as a cricketer.

Rudie took five wickets in a one-day international
against England. He played in the ICC Cricket World
Cup in 2003 and, later that year, in the Rugby World
Cup, where he played fly half. In addition, he is
a medical doctor and runs the Naankuse Foundation
Wildlife Sanctuary.

Is there no end to Rudie's talents?!

Burns Gets Burnt

Toulouse were leading Bath by just two points in a 2018 Champions Cup match. In the last minutes of the game, Bath were awarded a penalty – in front of the posts. The fans cheered. This was their moment to seize victory. It was in the bag!

Bath's full-back Freddie Burns stepped up to take the penalty kick. It was the sort of shot he would make 99 times out of 100. This was that other time! Freddie hit the post with his kick . . . and the home crowd groaned.

> **"How did he miss from there? But there's no time to dwell on that."**
> – commentator

Two minutes later, Semesa Rokoduguni made a searing break from deep within his own half. Bath piled forwards, sensing a chance for a try. Suddenly, Burns was through with the ball . . .

He ran forwards unopposed and crossed the try line, the ball held in one hand as he punched the air in celebration with the other. He had made up for his goal-kicking error moments earlier!

But instead of placing the ball down immediately, Freddie took four or five more paces to touch down under the posts. Big mistake . . .Toulouse winger Maxime Médard caught Freddie from behind and knocked the ball out of his hand. No try!

Freddie was subbed off and Toulouse won. He apologised to his team-mates and the fans afterwards. He'd learned an important lesson – never celebrate too early!

Surprise Shootout

Penalty shootouts, used to settle a match that's ended in a draw, are common in football but rare in rugby. A shootout was used to dramatically settle a 26–26 draw in the 2009 Heineken Cup semi-final clash between Leicester Tigers and Cardiff Blues. Leicester had seen a 26–12 lead slip away in the last minutes of normal time. Then, 20 minutes of extra time had failed to find a winner.

Penalties were taken from the 22-metre line and each side nominated their five best kickers – all backs.

After 14 penalties, the score was 6–6 and all the backs had taken their kicks. Penalties now had to be taken by the forwards, some of whom rarely ever kicked the ball. Martyn Williams missed his kick for

Cardiff, whilst Leicester forward Jordan Crane booted the ball over, winning the game for Leicester. Phew!

Going For Gold

Name: Portia Woodman

Born: Kawakawa, New Zealand, 1991

Country: New Zealand

Clubs: Auckland Storm, Kaikohe RFC, Northland Kauri

Position: Wing

Famous for: Exceptional speed, agility and try scoring ability, widely regarded as one of the best women's rugby sevens players in the world

In 2012, New Zealand rugby launched a nationwide search called Go4Gold. Its aim was to unearth new female talent in time for the 2016 Olympics, where sevens would debut as a medal sport. At the time, New Zealand did not have a women's sevens team.

Portia Woodman was a 21-year-old netballer, playing for the Northern Mystics. She decided to go along for the Go4Gold try-outs with her Mystics team-mate Kayla McAllister. Some 800 women attended trials all over New Zealand. Just 30 players were selected and these were then whittled down to 12. Amongst the dozen were Portia and Kayla.

The pair had to adjust from non-contact netball to the fast and furious world of sevens, where tackling, rucks and fend-offs are all part of the game. At least they had rugby experience in their families – Kayla's brother Luke played for the All Blacks, as did Portia's father, Kawhena, who also appeared in 126 matches for North Auckland.

> **"I think the most shocking part for me was having to get into the rucks. I wasn't quite used to getting my head banged around."**
>
> – Portia Woodman

In less than a year, the two women flew out to Russia to take part in the Sevens World Cup. New Zealand's fledgling sevens side conceded only one try in three group games and powered past England and Canada to win the competition. Portia, out on the wing, was the tournament's leading try scorer. She topped the try-scoring table again at the 2016 Sevens World Cup.

Portia's searing pace and nimble footwork, learned from netball, marked her out as a special talent, and in 2013 she was selected for New Zealand's 15-a-side team. Over the next decade, she successfully managed to juggle being a sevens star and a member of the Black Ferns.

In the 15-a-side code, Portia has scored a stunning 38 tries at a rate of more than one try per game. This includes an almost ridiculous 13 tries at the 2017 Women's Rugby World Cup, where New Zealand became world champions.

2022 proved a stellar year for Portia, who passed not one but two incredible landmarks. She became the first woman to score more than 200 tries in World

DID YOU KNOW?

Portia's medal haul with the New Zealand sevens team also includes a 2016 Olympic silver medal and a 2020 Olympic gold medal. Go, Portia!

Rugby Sevens Series. Then she bagged seven tries in a single match, as the Black Ferns thrashed Japan 95 – 12. This match was a warm-up for the big one, the 2021 Women's Rugby World Cup, delayed a year by the pandemic.

During the tournament, Portia broke the record for the most tries scored at Women's World Cups with 20 tries in just two tournaments. But far more important to her was that the Black Ferns overcame top sides such as France and England to be crowned champions again.

Dream Debuts

Dozens of players are 'one-cap wonders' – they get one chance to play for their country, then are never picked again. Others seize the chance to impress at a young age, like 18-year-old Tom Curry, who had a storming debut game versus Argentina in 2017.

Former England superstar Jonny Wilkinson and Sylvia Brunt who plays for the Black Ferns were also both 18 on their debut, whilst Beibhinn Parsons was two years younger when she was picked to play for the Irish women's team in 2018. In rugby league, Gemma Walsh was just 16 when she made her debut for Great Britain at the 2000 World Cup. Amazing!

Few young debutants could have had a better game than Wales's Keith Jarrett. Aged 18, and selected to play out of position as a full-back against England, he scored a try and a total of 19 points as Wales won. Australia's James O'Connor was just a year older when he scored three tries on his first full international versus Italy in 2009. And in rugby league, few can compete with Gavin Gordon, aged just 17, for a dream debut. In his first ever game for Ireland, he also scored a hat-trick of tries.

DID YOU KNOW?

Maro Itoje represented England at under-17 level . . . as a shot putter. He also played basketball before focusing on rugby. It was the right decision – he's been nominated for World Rugby Player of the Year three times already!

The Titans

Imagine having to train in the dark and play matches in secret at the dead of night. That's what happened in Greece, when rugby was banned!

From 2015, because of a dispute over who ran the game in Greece, rugby league was outlawed for many clubs and players – including those trying to form a national team called the Titans. Players who disobeyed the rules could end up in court. Secret matches were stopped by visits from the police. Crazy!

"Some of the boys have been in courthouses and police stations just for playing rugby league. We'd get called to help them with money for a lawyer."
– Steve Georgallis, Greece coach

In 2018, when Malta visited Greece to play a World Cup qualifying game, it ended up being more like a spy mission than a rugby match.

First, photos of the venue were posted on social media. It was a trick, though – to fool the police. This decoy venue was a seven-hour drive from where the game was *actually* being played.

But, owing to the secrecy, players from both sides didn't know where the game was to be held either! They got on buses without knowing where they needed to go . . .

Finally, the teams made it to the venue, a small stadium high in the mountains near Athens. There were no fans, only coaches and officials.

Greece's Titans defeated Malta 60–4. Further wins against Ukraine, Norway and Serbia saw them achieve their dream and reach the World Cup tournament for the very first time.

Happily, by the time the World Cup came round, the ban on rugby in Greece had been lifted.

"I'm proud and happy and a little bit emotional," said coach Steve, even though Greece had lost their three matches. His players were no longer breaking the law by playing and a brighter future for Greek rugby lay ahead.

Winning Wayne

In 2022, New Zealand Rugby announced Wayne Smith as head coach of their women's rugby team, the Black Ferns. Wayne certainly got off to a winning start as the team secured victory in all of their first 12 matches. He took them all the way to Eden Park, where they , and seeing them lifted the Women's Rugby World Cup at Eden Park in front of 42,579 excited fans.

The victory made Wayne a three-time world cup winner as a coach. He was the All Blacks assistant coach in 2011 and 2015 when they won the men's Rugby World Cup. Well done, Wayne!

Danny in Defence

In 2021, Super League veteran Danny Houghton became a record breaker. His Hull FC side was battling the Warrington Wolves in a 14–14 game that went into ten minutes of extra time. Danny was at his defensive best, making a world record 85 tackles during the match. It was no fluke. Of the top ten performances with most tackles in a match in Super League history, Danny claims five of them!

DID YOU KNOW?

Organisers of the sevens competition at the Tokyo Olympics devised a novel way of delivering the ball. It rode on a remote-controlled bus, which then flicked the ball onto the pitch between a set of mini goal posts fitted to the bus's roof!

Tackle Tie

At the 2021 Women's Rugby World Cup, two players tied for the most tackles made: Alex Callender of Wales and the aptly named French second row forward Madoussou Fall. Both players made 80 tackles during the tournament. In a sport for which ten or more tackles per game is good work, Alex's 80 tackles came in at an average of 20 per game – outstanding!

DID YOU KNOW?

No Frenchman had ever won the Six Nations Player of the Championship award until 2020, when live-wire scrum half Antoine Dupont seized the prize. He liked it so much, he won it again two years later!

Henry's in a Hurry

Henry Arundell is one of the fastest players in world rugby. It's thought that he can sprint 100 metres in less than 10.9 seconds. Rapid! The full-back (and occasional winger) has scored a series of sensational pitch-length tries, including during his debut for England U20s versus Scotland U20s in February 2022. Henry was made Man of the Match, following the 41–24 win.

Less than five months later, Henry found himself in Australia, making his England debut. The 19 year old came on to play the last seven minutes of a full Test match. The first time he received the ball, Henry burst through the tackles of two Australian defenders, rounded another opponent, James O'Connor, then dotted the ball down for a try. It was his very first touch of his very first game for England! Epic!

Six weeks later and he scored with his first touch of the new Premiership season, kicking and chasing the ball more than 50 metres to score for his club, London Irish. Once again, Henry was in a hurry – he'd only been on the pitch 40 seconds!

A year after his England U20s debut, Henry was called into action for his first ever Six Nations match, versus Italy. And guess what? He scored again, taking a pass from Alex Mitchell and diving over the line.

Henry takes a notebook to every game he plays. He's had the jotter since the age of ten and it's a bit tatty. Inside, he has written down all his goals, and the competitions he wants to play in – from U16s at the Wellington Festival to a Lions tour and the 2027 World Cup.

"It's not that I'll be gutted if I don't achieve all those stages, it's just that it reminds me of why I started playing rugby."

DID YOU KNOW?
Only two teams in the Six Nations have *never* won the wooden spoon for finishing last in the table – Ireland and England.

WELL PLAYED!

Our fast-paced tour of rugby's most exciting, inspiring and funny moments is at an end – but our book is not!

Turn the page to find a simple player's guide, a glossary plus a quiz to test your knowledge.

How to Play: Basics

Could YOU be the next Maro Itoje or Emily Scarratt? Maybe you're playing rugby already, at school or with a local team. But if you're new to the game, here are some basics to get you started . . .

The aim of rugby is to score more points than the opposing team by carrying, passing or kicking the ball into the opponent's in-goal area and grounding it (touching it onto the ground) for a try, or kicking it through the goal posts.

Teams consist of 15 players in rugby union and 13 players in rugby league (and seven players in the version of the game called sevens). Within a team, each player has a different position and role:

RUGBY POSITIONS AND NUMBERS
(rugby union)

FORWARDS

1. Tight-head prop
2. Hooker
3. Loose-head prop
4. Second row or Lock
5. Second row or Lock
6. Blindside flanker
7. Open side flanker
8. 'Number 8' or Lock

BACKS

9. Scrum-half (half back)
10. Fly half
11. Left wing
12. Inside centre
13. Outside centre
14. Right wing
15. Full-back

The game starts with a **kick-off** (one team kicking the ball to the other). The teams then try to gain possession of the ball and move it into their opponent's goal area. Players can run or kick the ball forward, but aren't allowed to pass it forward.

If a team does not have possession of the ball, there are several different ways to get it back:

Tackling – players can tackle their opponents by grabbing and bringing them to the ground. Tackles must be made below the shoulders and without using dangerous techniques. The player who is tackled must release the ball.

Rucks and mauls – a ruck or maul happens when a player is tackled. In a ruck, players from both teams bind together and try to take control of the ball with their feet. In a maul, opposition players use their hands to try to grab the ball from the player who has possession.

Scrums are formed when there is a minor infringement or the ball goes out of play. In a scrum, the forwards from each team bind together and try to hook the ball backward with their feet.

Line-outs are formed when the ball goes out of bounds. Players from both teams line up at right angles to the side line and a player from the team that didn't previously have possession throws it in. Players lift their team-mates to try to catch the ball.

There are several ways to score (the scores below are from rugby union – rugby league uses different scores):

Try (five points) – a player grounds (touches) the ball over the opposition goal line (or try line).

Conversion (two points) – after a player scores a try, their team can attempt a conversion kick, aiming the ball over the crossbar and between the goal posts.

Drop goal (three points) – a player can drop kick the ball through the goal from anywhere on the field and at any time.

Penalty kick (three points) – an attempt at goal may be awarded following a foul.

163

Types of play that must be avoided are called **fouls**. These include high tackles, other dangerous play and deliberate rule-breaking. A foul may result in a free kick, a penalty kick for the opposing team – or a yellow or red card being given to the player.

The game is supervised by a **referee**, who makes sure the rules are being followed and the players are safe at all times. They are helped by two touch judges, or assistant referees, who monitor the **goal line**.

DID YOU KNOW?

Of the two versions of the sport, rugby union is more widely played across the globe. Rugby league is popular in Australia, New Zealand and the UK – particularly in the north of England.

Rugby union versus rugby league

While many of the rules are the same between these two versions of the sport, there are some key differences:

Rugby union is played with 15 players per team. Rugby league is played with 13 players per team.

Scrums and line-outs are more complicated, and involve more players, in rugby union.

There are different rules for tackling, and resuming play, between the two games.

The scoring system is different too. For example, a try in rugby league is worth four points, but five in rugby union. A drop goal is worth one point in league and a penalty two points.

Glossary

ADVANTAGE When a team is allowed to continue play despite an infringement by the opposition. If the team benefits from the advantage, the game continues; if not, a penalty is awarded.

BACK A player, usually wearing a shirt numbered between 9 and 15, who don't typically take part in scrums and line-outs but are often known for their speed and agility, and are generally responsible for attacking and scoring.

BINDING The way that players grasp hold of each other to, safely and securely, to form a scrum, ruck or maul.

CONVERSION A kick at goal taken after a try.

DROP GOAL A kick taken in open play by dropping the ball and kicking it as it bounces off the ground.

FORWARD A player, usually wearing a shirt numbered between 1 and 8, who is often involved in the more physical elements of play, including scrums, line-outs, rucks and mauls.

FORWARD PASS When a player passes the ball to a team-mate in a forward direction. Forward passes are not allowed and result in a scrum for the opposing team.

FRONT ROW The three forwards – two props and hooker – which form the front of one team's pack when in a scrum.

HIGH TACKLE A tackle above the shoulders (or above the wait in some amateur rugby), which is considered dangerous play and is against the rules.

IN-GOAL AREA The area behind the try line where a player can ground the ball to score a try.

KNOCK-ON When a player accidentally drops the ball forward, resulting in a scrum being awarded to the opposing team.

LINE-OUT layers from both teams compete to catch the ball thrown from the side line. Line-outs are used to restart play after the ball crosses the side line (also known as going 'into touch').

MAUL After a tackle, players from both teams bind together to try to gain (or keep) possession of the ball.

OFFSIDE When a player is positioned in front of a team-mate who last played the ball or ahead of the ball when it was last kicked. Offside players cannot be involved with play.

PACK A group consisting of all the forwards, heading towards a scrum.

PENALTY A kick awarded to a team following a foul of offside by the opposition.

RUCK After a tackle, players from both teams bind together to try to gain (or keep) possession of the ball. Whereas players use their feet in a ruck, they use their hands in a maul.

RUGBY WORLD CUP (RWC) An international tournament played every four years.

SCRUM Eight players from each team bind together and compete to gain possession of the ball.

SEVENS A seven-a-side version of the sport, played at the Olympic Games.

SIN BIN When a player is temporary suspended for a short time, usually ten minutes, as punishment for a foul.

SIX NATIONS An annual tournament played between the national teams of England, Wales, Scotland, Ireland, France and Italy. There are both men's and women's competitions.

TACKLE When the player with the ball is stopped and brought to the ground by an opposing defender.

TEST A match between two national teams.

TRY When a player places the ball over the goal line in the opponent's in-goal area.

TRY LINE Another name for the goal line.

Test Your Knowledge

1. Which two countries are the only ones to win the men's Rugby World Cup three times?

2. How many players play in a rugby union team?

3. Which women's national team is called the Black Ferns?

4. Which England player excelled at the shot put, representing England internationally?

5. Who was the first Black British player to go on tour for England?

6. Who holds the record for the fastest try?

7. In which country was wheelchair rugby invented?

8. What was the profession of Ned Haig, who invented the game of sevens rugby?

9. Which two of these four players played in the first British women's rugby league team to tour abroad, in 1996: Brenda Dobek, Margaret Alphonsi, Caitlin Beevers, Lisa McIntosh?

10. Which national team is nicknamed the Brave Blossoms?

11. Which nation's rugby team is honoured on their country's seven-dollar banknote?

12. Who was the first woman to score 200 tries in the World Rugby Women's Sevens Series?

13. Which animal raced against South African star Byran Habana in 2007?

14. Which two teams compete in the Ashes competition?

Test Your Knowledge answers: 1. New Zealand and South Africa (page 27); **2.** 15 (page 13); **3.** New Zealand (page 28); **4.** Maro Itoje (page 84); **5.** Billy Boston (page 56); **6.** Tyson Lewis (page 101); **7.** Canada (page 40); **8.** Butcher (page 105); **9.** Brenda Dobek and Lisa McIntosh (page 96); **10.** Japan (page 21); **11.** Fiji (page 80); **12.** Portia Woodman (page 110); **13.** Cheetah (page 116); **14.** Great Britain and Australia (page 83)

Look out for more fun-filled books from Farshore!

Incredible Sports

Amazing Facts

Amazing Football Facts

CLIVE GIFFORD is an award-winning author of more than 200 books, including the official *Rugby World Cup Japan 2019™ Kids' Handbook*. His books have won the Blue Peter Children's Book Award, the Royal Society Young People's Book Prize, the School Library Association's Information Book Award and Smithsonian Museum's Notable Books For Children. Clive lives in Manchester but has watched rugby far and wide, from Sale to Singapore, Twickenham to Tahiti.

LU ANDRADE is an illustrator from Ecuador, currently living in the mountains of Quito. She has studied everything from cinematography to graphic design. After focusing on digital animation for four years, she turned her hand to illustration, working on projects including *Good Night Stories for Rebel Girls*.